# Top Answers to Job Interview Questions

*Donald K. Burleson*

*I dedicate this book to John Lavender for putting up with all my tantrums*

# Top Answers to Job Interview Questions

**By**: Donald K. Burleson

Printed in the United States of America.

Published by Rampant TechPress, Kittrell, North Carolina, USA

**Editors:** Andy Liles, John Lavender and Janet Burleson

**Production Editor:** Teri Wade

**Cover Design:** Bryan Hoff

**Illustrations**: Mike Reed

**Printing History:**

April, 2004 for First Edition

Many of the designations used by computer vendors to distinguish their products are claimed as Trademarks. All names known to Rampant TechPress to be trademark names appear in this text as initial caps.

Flame Warriors illustrations are copyright © by Mike Reed Illustrations Inc.

The information provided by the authors of this work is believed to be accurate and reliable, but because of the possibility of human error by our authors and staff, Rampant TechPress cannot guarantee the accuracy or completeness of any information included in this work and is not responsible for any errors, omissions, or inaccurate results obtained from the use of information in this work.

ISBN: 0-9744355-5-4

Library of Congress Control Number: 2004101892

# Index to Telephone Interview Top Answers

# Index to On-site Interview Top Answers

# Table of Contents

---

# Using the Online Code Depot

Your purchase of this book provides you with complete access to the online code depot that contains the sample questions and answers.

All of the job questions in this book are located at the following URL:

www.rampant.cc/job_top.htm

All of the sample tests and questions in this book will be available for download in a zip format, ready to use for your next interview.

If you need technical assistance in downloading or accessing the scripts, please contact Rampant TechPress at info@rampant.cc.

### Get the Advanced Oracle Monitoring and Tuning Script Collection

The complete collection from Mike Ault, the world's best DBA.

Packed with 590 ready-to-use Oracle scripts, this is the definitive collection for every Oracle professional DBA.

It would take many years to develop these scripts from scratch, making this download the best value in the Oracle industry.

It's only $39.95 (less than 7 cents per script!)

To buy for immediate download, go to
www.rampant.cc/aultcode.htm

# Conventions Used in This Book

It is critical for any technical publication to follow rigorous standards and employ consistent punctuation conventions to make the text easy to read.

However, this is not an easy task. Within any book, specific markers should be used to denote special areas of importance. To provide consistency and readability we will use the following conventions:

**?**    **Question: This is a question that you will want ask every interviewed candidate.**

   **I wonder? This is a question you may have about interviewing questions.**

   **Best Answer: This symbol will allow you to quickly access the best answer for the question.**

   **Hidden Agenda: This symbol alerts your real agenda behind the interview question.**

   **Trick Question: This indicates a question that can elicit incriminating information about the candidate.**

   **Bad Practice: This symbol denotes an inappropriate or illegal technique.**

# Acknowledgements

This type of highly technical reference book requires the dedicated efforts of many people. Even though we are the authors, our work ends when we deliver the content. After each chapter is delivered, several technical HR reviewers carefully review and correct the technical content.

After the technical review, experienced copy editors polish the grammar and syntax. The finished work is then reviewed as page proofs and turned over to the production manager, who arranges the creation of the online code depot and manages the cover art, printing distribution, and warehousing.

In short, the author played a small role in the development of this book, and we need to thank and acknowledge everyone who helped bring this book to fruition:

**John Lavender**, for the production management, including the coordination of the cover art, page proofing, printing, and distribution.

**Teri Wade**, for her help in the production of the page proofs.

**Andy Liles**, for his fantastic production coordination.

**Bryan Hoff**, for his exceptional cover design and graphics.

**Janet Burleson,** for her assistance with the overall management.

**Linda Webb**, for her expert clerical services.

# Preface

At the interviewing stage of the hiring process the real work begins. The interview serves to confirm that the candidate is "right" for the job, and this is a very subjective judgment. The person may have a pleasant demeanor or you may just have a "feeling" about them.

This is an indispensable guide to ensuring that you make the best possible hiring decision. The wrong decision can cost your company thousands of dollars in training expenses, or worse. For example, hiring an employee with a history of suing their employer may not be a good idea, yet few know how to find this information.

By the time the candidate arrives at the interview, you should have already conducted preliminary screenings of the résumé, job history and academic history and found the candidate to have the minimum qualifications for the job. Now comes the hard part.

The interview is always the make-or-break test of a manager. You must understand the dynamics of the job interview and the multitude of ways job candidates will try to impress or deceive you.

Successful interviewing requires both knowledge and tact, and the savvy managers know the right questions to ask and the hidden meanings behind the answers. Often the important hiring information is either illegal or inappropriate. Knowing whether a female employee has small children at-home can affect their attendance, lying on the résumé or during the interview can indicate moral turpitude. You must learn how to assess the candidate in innocent and unobtrusive ways so that you can get the data you need to choose the perfect person for the job.

In their effort to find employment, candidates will try all sorts of deceptive practices from feigning an outgoing personality to faking qualifications. You must learn to spot these fakers and send them on their way quickly and legally.

The following chapters provide both strong and weak answers to both pointed and open-ended questions so that you can find important information in a subtle way and without violating the law. Best of all, this book contains important questions that every candidate should ask during the job interview.

My qualifications for this book are unique. I'm the author of over 30 books and a seasoned hiring manager with a degree in Social Psychology and an MBA. As result of my education and experience doing hundreds of interviews, I have extremely good "radar", a gut feeling about a job applicant that is usually correct.

This book is my way to share the tricks and techniques that I have used over the past 20 years to help companies find the perfect person for the job.

## Key Features

This book is unique because it provides the top answers to the most probing questions and allows you to get insights into hidden perils and pitfalls. The book also includes the questions that every good candidate should ask you during your interview, and more importantly, the questions that they should never ask.

- Implement your hidden agenda without breaking the law.

- Master the interpersonal evaluation aspect of the job interview.

- Learn how the perfect candidate should handle open-ended and ambiguous questions.

- Know the questions that every good candidate will ask.

- See the top answers to your interview questions.

- Tell when an interview candidate is lying.

Let's get started with a discussion about the job interviewing process and how you can prepare to ace your on-site meeting.

# Employer Interview Preparation

## Introduction

In today's highly volatile work environment, the average employee rarely stays with a single employer for a long period of time. While some attrition is inevitable, there are many techniques that savvy managers can use to hire and retain top talent.

Generally, the selection of an employee is accomplished in the following phases:

- Initial screening of résumés by the HR department (keyword scan).

- Non-Technical telephone screening by the manager

- In-depth technical assessment by a senior technical person

- On-site interview (check demeanor, personality, and attitude)

- Background check (verify employment history, education, certifications, criminal history)

- Determine salary, benefits and prepare a written job offer

As we can see, by the time the candidate is invited for an interview he/she has already passed several pre-screening tests.

While the recent recession has created a shakeout within the lower ranks of employees, there are still opportunities for those that excel at their duties. Your goal is to make sure that your interviewer correctly identifies this type of employee.

---

## The Employers Preparation

By the time you have invited a candidate to interview, you have narrowed your list to the top-n candidates. For each top-n applicant, background checks on their résumé, academic history, and work history should be completed. Interviewing is very time-consuming and you must weed-out those with fraudulent résumé items.

Because you have reviewed each applicant's résumé, it's a good idea to prepare a list of job interview questions that are designed specifically for each candidate. Let's start by reviewing how you should review the material on each résumé.

*"Yes, I know Java, J2EE and two other computer words."*

# Trash the bad Résumés

The evaluation of the résumé is a critical part of the selection process. In a tight job market, it is not uncommon to receive hundreds of résumés, and it is your job to fairly and efficiently pre-screen applicants and narrow-down a short-list of qualified individuals for a detailed interview.

When evaluating hundreds résumés, you must quickly eliminate unprofessional applicants. Some of the most common criteria for trashing a résumé include:

**Too Wordy** – The purpose of the résumé is to get an interview, nothing more. One page per decade of experience is best.

**Bad grammar/spelling** – Résumés with typos and poor grammar are immediately rejected.

**Too personal** – Adding a photo or an extensive description of your personal life is inappropriate, in poor taste, and indicates an unprofessional applicant. The right résumé is tight, concise and on-focus.

Let's start by looking at techniques for evaluating the job history component.

## Evaluating Employment History

Evaluation of a job candidate's work history is the single most critical factor in résumé screening. Candidates without significant work history may spend an undue amount of time learning their jobs, while a more expensive, experienced candidate may be a better overall value for the hiring company.

When screening a résumé, many managers use rules like these:

**High Work Quality** - Remember, not all experience is equal in value. Many demanding workplaces provide excellent training and experience, while others provide only glancing exposure to state-of-the-art technical and job issues.

**No Exaggeration** - Regardless of the internal strength of a résumé it is critical that you verify that the applicant did not "puff" their responsibilities or add fraudulent education or honors to their list of qualifications.

**Evidence of Enthusiasm** – Attitude is often as important as skills, and a go-getter is always regarded highly. The savvy applicant will spin their work history to show ambition, drive, and obsessive nature.

Now let's look at some of the most common question that hiring managers have about the résumé evaluation process. Having looked at many thousands of résumé's, there are several important screening factors that must be considered.

"Yes, I was an NCAA Basketball All-star"

*Don't get caught in a lie.*

> 🗣️ **Should I eliminate someone who has slightly exaggerated their qualifications?**

In the soft market of the early twenty-first century, it is not uncommon for a desperate job applicant to forge a work history with a defunct company and assume that you will not be able to verify the employment. Because of the rampant fraud, you must become more sophisticated and take the time to perform cursory background checks that will reveal any inflated job duties, false degrees, and other onerous résumé items.

Fortunately, "experience puffing" and résumé fraud are very easy to detect. In a typical job solicitation and savvy résumé reviewer can easily toss-out up to 30% of the résumés as being clearly fraudulent, and the detailed background check preceding the on-site interview will surely reveal any inaccuracies in the remaining résumés.

For example, an applicant might claim they had a lead management role in a project when they were actually just managing a small component of the project. While their prior employer will only provide their salary, job description, and date of employment, it is very easy to contact their former co-workers and supervisors. Many managers have their own lingo to get their message across without violating disclosure laws.

For example, personal opinions are exempt and some managers might say something like "I would not hire them again," or other statements of opinion.

The best candidate will present all of their salient experience and avoid the temptation to "puff" their responsibilities.

*"I'm seeking an executive position that is commensurate with my skills."*

💻 **Code Depot Username = reader, Password = micki**

☠ **Exercise Caution with unverifiable Résumé Items**

The explosion of competition in the market has led to conditions where some overseas workers present résumé items noting overseas jobs and Universities.

You have the unique challenge of verifying employment history with a company that no longer exists, a University without a phone number or mailing address, or job references that cannot speak English.

In recent years the proliferation of phony résumés has become extremely problematic. In many cases, the hiring manager strongly discounts résumés where the employment and educational history cannot be accurately verified. Many HR departments, frustrated with confirming overseas employment and academic histories, never forward these types of résumés to the hiring manager.

 **How will I check personal history?**

Almost all employers perform a background check, which is easily obtained via national services (www.ussearch.com) and private detective agencies. In many cases, a routine background check can reveal acts of moral turpitude such as slow payments and shirking of debts. You can easily get a full report on many areas of your short-list candidate's personal life including:

- Arrest and criminal conviction record
- Academic transcripts (supplied as an "official" transcript)
- Credit history
- Records of civil lawsuits

It is within your right to require that a candidate not have any criminal convictions except minor traffic violations.

You will also be aware of all arrests from the public records even if the candidate was never convicted. Legally you may not consider arrests without convictions, but you can always eliminate the résumé claiming some other deficiency. Many managers who reject arrested candidates simply claim that they feel that the candidate would not be a good fit.

*You cannot always identify drug users*

In a tight and selective job market, many companies want employees to demonstrate the highest degree of personal and moral integrity. Acts of moral turpitude such as a history of drug usage, dishonesty, lying, cheating, or theft may be grounds for immediate rejection.

> **Can I gain access to confidential information about a candidate?**

You are within your rights to ask all applicants to sign a waiver allowing previous employers to disclose personal information and in some cases you may ask the applicant to submit to a polygraph exam.

The waiver to disclose personal information can be used to get medical records (especially records of treatment for drug abuse and psychiatric history), records from psychologist and counselor visits, and other types of confidential information that is not available to the general public.

Of course, the candidate has the right to refuse to sign the release, but this can sometime be perceived as self-incriminating.

You should always check with an attorney before requiring candidates to sign a personal or medical waver because state and local laws may prohibit this practice.

## Evaluating Academic History

While a formal education is not always a predictor of success at a job, there can be no doubt that job candidates with advanced degrees from respected universities possess both the high intelligence and persistence needed into succeed in a professional environment.

However, not all schools are created equal. You should evaluate every résumé for the quality of the major. The school should be evaluated for its' quality, accreditation, and selectivity in student admissions.

There are a huge number of poor schools, and you may want to discount schools that offer academic credit for life experiences, require no classroom participation, or require no entrance qualifications.

This is a major problem especially with MBA programs, and in most cases a quick Google search will reveal the less-than-stellar degree programs. For MBAs, some employers require that the school be accredited by the *American Assembly of Collegiate Business Schools* (AACSB), the accrediting body for many mainstream US universities.

Online resources such as US New and World Report – America's Best Colleges and the Gourman Report are excellent tools for evaluating academic quality. However, you must always require an official transcript before hiring any employee.

---

### How much weight should I assign to the quality of the College degree?

---

When evaluating the educational background of job candidates, it is important to remember that colleges vary widely in their screening requirements and academic quality. Some hiring managers tend to select candidates from top tier colleges and universities because they rely on the universities to do the pre-screening for them.

For example, a professional who has been selected by a top tier university clearly demonstrates high achievement, high intelligence, and a very strong work ethic.

At the other end of the spectrum, there are many job candidates who have attended vocational schools, night schools, and non-accredited universities who receive bachelor's degrees in non-traditional study areas such as Astrology. In many cases, these professionals may lack the necessary technical and communicational skills required to succeed in some highly-technical industries.

The type of degree (BA, BS) and the College major is also a factor in the suitability of the job candidate.

---

Many employers will save time by letting universities pre-screen their job candidates. For example, MIT carefully screens grades and achievement. This pre-screening by the university allows companies to choose computer science professionals with increased confidence in the candidate's required skills.

## Rating your College Education

Many employers hire a professional agency to evaluate educational background while other functional managers take it upon themselves to evaluate the quality of the job candidate's formal education. Fortunately, sources for rating colleges and universities can easily be found online.

Some of the larger corporations prefer that the job candidate's degree be from a university possessing a first-ticr or second-tier rating by *US News & World Report's "America's Best Colleges"* or degrees from exceptional universities (as listed in the *Gourman Report*).

Of course, not all jobs duties require a college degree. For lower-level jobs the formal academic requirements are less challenging, but the lead departmental employee in a large corporation must possess high intelligence, superb communication skills, and the drive and persistence that is most commonly associated with someone who has taken the time to invest in a quality education.

For example, a BS or MS in Computer Science generally requires the job candidate to have a very strong theoretical background in mathematics and physics. Those with formal degrees in computer science tend to gravitate toward software engineering and software development fields that require in-depth knowledge about lower-level components in computer systems.

On the other hand, we see the BS and MBA degrees in Information Systems. Those degrees offered by accredited business colleges (AACSB) tend to strike a balance between computer programming skills and business skills. The information systems degree candidate will have a background in systems analysis and design, as well as familiarity with functional program development for specific business processes.

 **How important is the College major?**

There is a great deal of debate about what academic majors, if any, are valid indicators of future success in a professional position. However, it is well documented that different majors attract students with varying abilities.

Studies that correlate the Graduate Records Exam (GRE) scores with academic major confirm that higher GRE scores are associated with majors such as Engineering, Computer Science and Business Administration, while students with major such as Physical Education and Astrology tend to have lower average GRE scores.

The following list describes some indicators used in large corporations for assessing the relative value of different college majors:

- **Engineers**. Engineers tend to make great computer professionals, especially those with degrees in Electrical Engineering (EE). An engineering curriculum teaches logical thinking and data structure theory that makes it easy for the engineer to learn new tasks quickly.

  However, while engineers have unimpeachable technical skills, their oral and written communication skills are often lacking. Therefore, functional managers should pay careful attention to communication skills when interviewing job applicants with engineering degrees.

- **Business Majors**. Business majors make excellent system developers and analysts because of their training in finance, accounting, marketing, and other business processes. Many business schools also require matriculated students to take several courses in Information Technology. Not all college business schools are equal, though.

When screening a job applicant with a business major, the manager should check to ensure that the degree is from a business school accredited by the American Assembly of Collegiate Business Schools (AACSB). There are many fly-by-night business schools, and their depth of training may be vastly different.

- **Computer Science Majors**. Computer scientists typically receive four years of extensive technical training, and are ideal candidates for computer jobs requiring in-depth technical ability. However, like the engineers, many computer scientists have sub-standard communications skills.

- **Music Majors**. For many years, IBM recruited from the ranks of college musicians because hiring managers found that musicians possessed ability in logical thinking that made them ideal candidates for IT skills training.

- **Math Majors**. Math majors tend to possess excellent logical thinking skills and often possess a background in computer science. Like many quantitative majors, social and communications skills may be a concern.

*Some computer professionals are insecure about their vocabulary*

- **Education Majors**. Evaluation of education majors is extremely difficult because of the wide variation in quality between universities. Nationally, GRE test rankings by academic major show that education majors consistently rank in the lowest 25% of knowledge.

# How to Review Personal History

Almost all large companies use their HR department to conduct a check of all publicly-available records about every short-list candidate. These records include:

- Public criminal records

- Public Civil court records

- Credit check

These background checks can be done without the candidates' knowledge or consent.

Remember, lying during an interview is sure way to remove a candidate from contention. For example, if you have prior knowledge of a candidates' criminal history you can test the candidates' honesty by asking *"Have you ever been convicted of any crime, other than a motor vehicle violation?"*

Savvy candidates know about public records and will be completely forthright and honest with all questions about their personal history, even if the question is illegal. See Chapter 7 for methods to elicit illegal information from a candidate without breaking the letter of the law. If asking an illegal question is challenged in court, make sure you document the other reasons you chose not to hire that candidate.

Let's take a closer look at the information you should have about each candidate prior to the interview.

## Should I ignore a DUI arrest because they were found not guilty?

As we have noted, there are many services that can instantly retrieve all criminal records about a candidate, including all arrests, even if they were not convicted. These records may include both arrests and convictions, and most cost less than $100, making the criminal check a due-diligence task for almost all employers.

You are prohibited from using arrest information against an applicant, but you can rest assured that it is almost impossible for a candidate to prove that you used this information against them.

---

*Drinking problems can cause unpredictable mood swings.*

Remember, criminal records are public record and you do not need the candidate's knowledge or consent to conduct a criminal history search.

If the candidate has a history of criminal activity while less than 18 years of age the court records are usually sealed and cannot be disclosed without their express consent. However, civil lawsuits resulting from criminal actions of a minor are public record, and while a criminal conviction for vandalism may be sealed, the resulting lawsuit against their parents is public record.

Using online background reports, you can quickly and easily get a complete criminal history, including all charges and whether they resulted in a conviction.

*"I'm holding-out for a senior management position."*

Here is an actual sample from a criminal background check. Note the high level of detail, with complete dates, charges and outcomes.

| | |
|---|---|
| Subject | ROBERT SCUMBAG |
| Race | White |
| Sex | Male |
| Date of Birth | **/**/1966 |
| Height | 74 INCHES |
| Weight | 310 POUNDS |
| Hair Color | BROWN |
| Eye Color | BLUE |
| Address | LIZARD LICK NC 27531 |

### Case 1 Details

| | |
|---|---|
| Case Number | 01928VF 027253 |
| Jurisdiction | NC |
| County | RALEIGH |
| Charge Class | Felony |
| Offense | POSSESS HEROIN |
| Statute | 90-95(D)(1) |
| Sentence | 6 MONTHS COUNTY JAIL |
| Fine Amount | 40,000.00 |
| Disposition Date | 08/06/1989 |
| Disposition | PROSECUTION COMPLETED |
| Amended Charge Class | N/A |
| Amended Charge Description | POSSESS HEROIN |

### Case 2 Details

| | |
|---|---|
| Case Number | 01FF3BF 027253 |
| Jurisdiction | NC |
| County | CHARLOTTE |
| Charge Class | Felony |
| Offense | POSSESS MARIJUANA UP TO 5 LBS |
| Statute | 90-95(D)(4) |
| Sentence | 2 YEARS PRISON |

| Fine Amount | N/A |
|---|---|
| Disposition Date | 08/06/1991 |
| Disposition | DEFERRED PROSECUTION |

| Case 3 Details | |
|---|---|
| Case Number | 6354242F j35342d |
| Jurisdiction | NC |
| County | RALEIGH |
| Charge Class | Felony |
| Offense | POSSESS STOLEN PROPERTY |
| Statute | 440-462(Z)(1) |
| Sentence | TWO YEARS CHAIN GANG |
| Fine Amount | N/A |
| Disposition Date | 08/06/1994 |
| Disposition | PROSECUTION COMPLETE |

| Case 4 Details | |
|---|---|
| Case Number | 6354242F j35342d |
| Jurisdiction | NC |
| County | RALEIGH |
| Charge Class | Felony |
| Offense | ASSAULT W DEADLY WEAPON |
| Statute | 230-23(D)(41) |
| Sentence | DISMISSED |
| Fine Amount | N/A |
| Disposition Date | 02/17/1998 |
| Disposition | DEFERRED PROSECUTION |

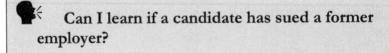 **Can I learn if a candidate has sued a former employer?**

In addition to immediate access to criminal history you can also get instant access to pubic records of civil litigation. Civil court checks involve all matters of public record including divorces, real estate transactions, and civil lawsuits.

These public records can be very revealing about a candidate's personality and predilection to enter a lawsuit, which is very important if you are trying to minimize liability. However, remember that you should check with an attorney before using this information to reject a candidate.

Some hiring managers are concerned when a candidate has a history of suing a previous employer for problems at the workplace, such as sexual harassment or unfair treatment.

You should always checked publicly-available civil records, either before of after your on-site interview.

 **Can I find out about immoral activity?**

Some employers conduct a credit history check, especially when the job involves access to liquid assets. Credits checks are available using online services such as Equifax, Experian, and TransUnion. While you may not be able to legally discriminate against a candidate for irresponsible financial dealings, you may be able to find out about:

**Poor payment history** – If the candidate has a history of late payments, it might relate to their personal integrity and commitment to obligations.

**Default on payment** – Stiffing creditors is considered immoral by some employers even though some laws may prohibit you from considering this information. Keep in mind that the candidate will see a record of any queries to their credit when they order a personal credit report.

With regard to bankruptcy, a lending institution may not hold a prior bankruptcy against someone after seven years, but it may be valuable information for you. Remember, you can use any reason (or no reason at all) for rejecting any job application.

Now that we understand how you must prepare, let's look at how you should prepare your agenda for each on-site interview.

# Your Hidden Agenda

CHAPTER **2**

## How Not to Ask the Important Questions

There are many things that you may need to know about a job candidate, but cannot ask.  Family, financial, and personal issues may all have bearing on your hiring decision.  While these issues may be very important to you, you are prevented (both by anti-discrimination and decorum) from asking personal questions.

Some employers have concerns about a job candidate's personal life that cannot be easily answered during an interview.  These questions might include:

- **Will small children cause lost work time?** – She wears a wedding band, and she is young.  Will she quit in two-years to have children?  If so, we may not want to invest in training her.

- **Does he have family root in our area?**  People relocating to a new area exclusively for a job often get homesick and quit after a relatively short period of time.  If an applicant has family in the area they are likely to stay longer.

- **Will she fit in?**  We are a small community of Southern Baptists, and a non-Christian may not feel welcome in our small town.

- **Will he like our climate?**  He is from Miami and we need to know if he will be able to tolerate our dark cold winters in Anchorage.

- **Can he handle stress?** If he falls-apart during the first crisis, he might quit, or worse yet, go out on medical disability.

*For some workers, everything is an emergency!*

- **Does she smoke?** If we hire a cigarette smoker, the medical insurance rates for all of our employees may go up.

- **Will he shave?** We are a bank, and everyone must be clean-shaven. Will he be willing to forgo his moustache if we offer him this job, or sue us for making facial hair a job requirement?

- **Is she too old?** Her résumé is not clear about her actual age, and we don't want to hire someone over 50. If we hire someone over age 50, they will be eligible to retire at age 65. We would have to pay a lifetime retirement pension to someone with less than 15 years of service and the other employees with longer service records and no retirement benefits will be outraged.

- **Will she wear skirts?** We want all of our employees to dress in conservative business attire. We prefer that women wear tailored dresses or dress suits and that men wear a suit and tie. Will she agree to the dress code or give us legal trouble?

- **Will he start at-work relationships?** We lost our last manager just because he dated the woman in the shipping department. When they broke up, he quit and we lost a huge amount of money re-training a replacement. We don't want that to happen again.

- **Does she already have small children at home?** The other woman we hired had five small kids, and she looses more than 10 hours a week taking them to the doctor, and shuttling them to day care. We don't want someone who will be encumbered with non-work responsibilities.

- **Will his religion effect work performance?** Sometimes he will need to be available during holidays. A non-Christian would be a much better fit for us because we often do system maintenance during Christian holidays.

As you can see, these concerns are very delicate, but very real. The answers to these questions may be a deciding factor in the hiring decision. They are questions that may be answered using special questions designed to elicit the information in a legal and roundabout way.

There are many other personality and work-related questions for which you might seek answers.

- How well do they handle stress?
- Are they likely to be unsatisfied with the job?
- How long will they stay with us?
- Would they cause problems in the workplace?

By formulating a hidden agenda behind legitimate questions you can provide the candidate an opportunity to volunteer this critical information in an appropriate and non-threatening way.

Every hiring manager always uses a hidden agenda and seasoned managers are adept at disguising their real agenda behind seemingly innocuous questions. It is your challenge to find innocent and innocuous questions that will get the applicant to volunteer the desired information.

In later chapters we will denote hidden agenda questions with this marker:

 **Hidden Agenda: This symbol alerts you to the real agenda behind an interview question**

This will be your signal that the question has a hidden value and is designed to allow you to get information that is not readily apparent from the résumé and too delicate to ask directly.

Next, let's examine techniques for evaluating the personality of the job applicant. As any manager can attest, job qualifications are of little value if the employee does not possess the interpersonal and social skills to work effectively with co-workers.

# Evaluating Personality

What is more important to managers, technical knowledge or personality? Many times, managers concentrate too much on technical skill, and a candidate's personality is overlooked, often with disastrous results.

*Employees with immature personalities can cause tension at work.*

## Personality Traits

Almost every job involves interacting with co-workers, customers, and managers and social skills are sometimes as

---

important as qualifications. With that in mind, the following professional personality traits are, or ought to be, embodied by your ideal job candidate.

*A self-aware employee sees reality clearly.*

Regardless of the type of job, you want employees who are self-confident, curious, tenacious, polite, motivated, and a stickler for details. Let's take a closer look at these traits.

## Self-confidence

Employees who lack self-confidence might ask your opinion on every decision, no matter how large or small, and show no initiative. This indecision may be acceptable for a new employee working under the supervision of a senior employee, but the employee must learn to depend on their own judgment for important decisions. Nobody likes an employee who must be micro-managed.

In interviews, hypothetical questions must be asked about job-related problems with pointed questions about how the applicant would resolve the problem.

## A Curious Nature

Curiosity is a core trait of the employee in a dynamic work environment because the duties are constantly changing. Inflexible workers will be unable to cope. An employee who is not curious is usually passive and waits for problems to occur, reacting to each problem as it happen. On the other hand, a curious employee is proactive and will take measures to find problems and suggest enhancements before a problem occurs.

The curious employee is also motivated and may invest their personal money to stay current with their job technology. In interviews with potential employees, questions should be asked about the books and subscriptions the candidate relies upon to stay current in their field. Needless to say, answers indicating sole reliance on "the documentation set" are not an indication of professional curiosity.

*Motivation is a major factor in successful hiring.*

Employers value self-starting employees who require little supervision. In addition, successful employees prevent fires before they start, and smart employees know what things can cause trouble if they are ignored.

## A Tenacious Disposition

For many industry positions, a bulldog-like tenacity is required for troubleshooting problems. The employee should enjoy knuckling down on a problem and not giving up until an answer is found.

Drive and dedication are highly prized in the workplace and it is not uncommon to see the candidate who is more ambitious and goal-oriented secure a job over more technically qualified candidates.

## Polite Manners

An employee usually must work closely with other people and must show tact and interpersonal skills when dealing with subordinates, co-workers, and managers.

But, here's a fact of employee life. Project managers, developers, and users may sometimes appear with unreasonable requests or have impossible deadlines. Tact and interpersonal skills are required to respond to such requests without burning bridges.

## Detail Orientation

Being detail-oriented is perhaps the most important trait for any employee. Good employees for highly-technical positions are often described as having an "anal" personality, (after Sigmund Freud's theory of anal-retentive personalities) and have high attention to detail.

*Attention to Detail is critical for many jobs.*

A detail-oriented job candidate is usually early for an appointment and brings a PDA or calendar to an interview. Questions asked by the detail-oriented person are reflections of their research conducted on the potential new employer.

Next, let's examine some of the ways that savvy hiring managers get personality information from a job candidate.

## The Scientist Employee

The scientist employee is brilliant and sometimes shy, hates disorder, chaos, and conundrums, and greatly enjoys diving into the internal details of their job.

*Any employee who is fluent in Klingon may have a personality disorder.*

The scientist employee tends to have a love of music and gravitates towards degrees in "pure" College majors such as History, English, Math, or Physics.

Scientist employees usually keep their offices neat and orderly, with everything in its proper place. Common indicators of the scientist employee may include:

- **Attention to detail** - Scientist employees like order in every area of their lives and their database is no exception. They miss nothing, and pride themselves on their close attention to every detail of their jobs.

- **High professional standards** - The scientist employee believes that everything can be described with mathematical equations and every assertion can be proven with experimentation. The scientist employee hates "rules-of-thumb" and revels in finding exceptions to any general assertion.

- **Highly reliable** - The scientist employee is very careful and meticulous and will always justify every change in procedures (often with extraordinary detailed experimental evidence) before implementing anything new.

- **Extremely eloquent** - Some, (but not all) of the scientist employees can be identified by their grandiloquent prose. These employees love to use obscure words and complex verbal syntax, and normally keep an *Oxford English Dictionary* (OED) close at-hand. They love puns and double meanings, and enjoy using obscure words that have not been popular since the early 1800s.

*Nit-picky employees make great accountants!*

# The "Gung-Ho" Employee

The Gung-Ho employee is generally characterized by a "can-do" attitude. They are always bright and outgoing, and they always seem to be in a hurry. They tend to be impatient (especially with stupid questions), and they never "suffer fools gladly."

Even though their office is in complete chaos (with stacks of paper two-feet deep, and post-it notes cluttering the walls), they amaze visitors by being able to find exactly what they need within seconds. The Gung-Ho employee likes stimulants, and may drink volumes of coffee, keep lots of candy and sweets on their desk, and may be a chain smoker.

*Not all employees will work nights!*

The Gung-Ho employee is often a pragmatist and prefers experiential learning over theory. They gravitate toward degrees in "real-world" majors such as Computer Science, Engineering, or Business Administration. The Gung-Ho employee is competitive and may love sports, especially one-on-one competitive engagements such as golf or tennis. Their motto is, "Anything worth doing is worth doing to excess." Characteristics of the Gung-Ho employee may include:

- **Highly creative** - The Gung-Ho employee likes to think "outside the box," and often develops novel approaches to solving employee problems. The Gung-Ho employee loves new things, and may have a history of causing disruptions while implementing new and exciting techniques. They love to try new approaches, and if left to their own devices, they will spend all day thinking about ways to improve work processes.

- **Highly dedicated** - Gung-Ho employees always excel at their jobs, and they take every employee certification exam that has ever been offered. Their job is the most important aspect of their lives, and they are first to volunteer to work on Thanksgiving and Christmas.

- **Strategic orientation** - The Gung-Ho employee is more concerned with long-term results than operational details. The Gung-Ho employee relies more on heuristics (rules-of-thumb) than experimentation, and does not like to "waste time" experimenting with hypothetical issues.

- **Highly productive** - If you are on a deadline and have a problem requiring a Herculean effort, the Gung-Ho employee can be counted upon to get the job done on-time and under budget.

## The "Empathic" Employee

The Empathetic employee is outgoing, friendly, and reminds you of your favorite Aunt or Uncle. Being people-oriented, the Empathetic employee is more concerned with the social aspects of the job and loves to participate in group activities with co-workers.

The Empathetic employee is sometimes lacking in technical skills, but most co-workers don't care because they are such nice people. The Empathetic employee makes a great manager and is highly skilled at team building and is very tolerant of the shortcomings of co-workers.

Empathetic employees tend to gravitate toward people-oriented majors such as Psychology, Sociology, or Education. Their hobbies may include working with animals (dog showing), or volunteering with civic organizations. They like sports that include team activities such as soccer, but avoid one-on-one confrontation sports. Their motto is *"No one ever wrote on their tombstone I wish I had spent more time at the office."*

Characteristics of the Empathetic employee include:

- **Charming** - You cannot help but like the Empathetic employee. They are generally extroverted and always sensitive to the feelings of others. Empathetic employees make great bosses because they care more about ensuring that you spend quality time with your family than getting a project done on time.

- **Technically stable** - Empathetic employees have no great interest in new technologies and are content to keep their area stable. In multiple employee shops, they feel no need to compete with the other employees.

- **Modest** - The Empathetic employee may get certifications, but they will never have employee certificates hanging on their wall because they are concerned that their co-workers may think that they are being pretentious. Even if they win prestigious awards, they appear almost embarrassed about any public recognition.

- **Values family over work** - The Empathetic employee places family above employee work in importance. They sometimes refuse to work evenings or weekends, and cannot understand why anyone would devote their whole life to their job.

 **Can I require a personality test?**

Yes. There are many personality characteristics that can be accurately identified and measured. Personality tests will also identify neurotic and mentally-ill job applicants.

Personality disorders cost employers billions of dollars each year in lost productivity and many HR departments are now requiring paper-and-pencil personality tests to ensure that their new hires do not possess any mental disorder that might interfere with their ability to be productive.

In order to require a personality test you must be able to show that the test results are valid and that the results accurately predict future work performance. For this reason, many employers do not use psychological testing, but the tests are worth reviewing because they will give you insight into the types of personality characteristics that employers are seeking for specific types of jobs.

Some hiring managers swear by personality tests and claim that if you undertake the expense of using personality tests that you will be able to screen-out job candidates who are not likely to be successful at the job and to rank-order those candidates who are likely to be successful.

Let's take a look at the most important of the personality tests to understand how personality may affect your hiring decision.

# Using the MMPI

The most widely recognized personality test is the *Minnesota Multiphasic Personality Inventory* (MMPI). This is a 500 question true-false test that accurately evaluates personality characteristics along many dimensions, evaluating each personality factor on a scale from normal to neurotic to psychotic.

This test has been given to hundreds of thousands of people over many decades and the results are extremely accurate. MMPI results are so reliable that they are accepted in courts of law and are used to make important decisions about the mental state of criminals.

The MMPI has several scales, which are personality dimensions, each measuring a specific trait. Let's take a closer look at these scales and see how you may be able to use their data to screen job applicants.

## Lie scale

The lie scale measure honesty by asking questions in several forms and ascertaining whether you are deliberately attempting to deceive. Of course, a high score on the lie scale may constitute grounds for removal from consideration.

This scale is extremely accurate and many managers will deliberately ask question from the lie scale in order to determine your honesty.

## Hypochondriac scale

Concerns over bodily functions may be a sign of neurosis that may impact on-the-job performance. For example, a hypochondriac may have unfounded concerns over work-related environmental issues and also run-up huge medical bills.

## Depression scale

While clinical depression is a highly-treatable illness, many who suffer from depression fail to seek treatment. Obviously, a depressed employee will work slower and with more errors than a non-depressed employee.

While high score on the depression scale may indicate a suicidal candidate, low scores on the depression scale are also of serious concern. A low-level depressed employee may be likely to find they are unhappy with their job situation, and have a far higher propensity to quit than a non-depressed employee. Hence, all managers attempt to gauge the overall "attitude" of the job seeker, especially in jobs that require a large investment in training.

## Paranoia scale

The paranoid employee tends to have suspicion of others, a rigid belief system, and high sensitivity to criticism. People who score high in paranoia may make excellent attorneys and there are many jobs where having a "they are out to get me" attitude can be very beneficial.

## Hysteria scale

This is a very important scale for determining an employee's ability to handle stressful situations. High scores on the hysteria scale indicate a personality type who is likely to fall-apart when the job becomes stressful, functioning poorly, and sometimes requiring medical leave.

Interestingly, the scores for Hysteric correlate to gender, education-level, and social class. Statistically, women tend to score higher then men, and well-educated applicants tend to score higher then those without a College education. Those from wealthier social classes also tend to score higher then the blue-collar classes.

The savvy manager knows how to spot job candidates who may have hysterical tendencies and uses unobtrusive questions to get an idea of the capacity to handle stress.

## Social Introversion scale

This measures an applicants tendency to be shy, introverted and to withdraw from responsibilities. Those with low social introversion scores excel at jobs that involve working with the public such as sales and consulting. People with high scores on social introversion may do well at low-contact jobs such as computer programming.

## Hypomania scale

The hypomania scale measures low-grade manic-depressive traits, and manic behavioral disorders. The manic employee may have periods of very high productivity followed by periods of abject depression, combined with feelings of low self-worth.

## Psychasthenia scale

This scale measures unreasonable fears (phobias) and obsessive-compulsive problems. People who score high on this scale tend to have feelings of guilt combined with self-critical behavior. They are often poor workers, having difficulty concentrating and working with others.

---

### Machiavellianism scale

The Machiavellian scale is named after the stealthy and manipulative main character in the book *The Prince*. The company may want someone who is Machiavellian because they want someone with a manipulative personality who can connive and posture in order to get important work completed. Other employers may want a conformist who will not question the rules and obey blindly and without question or personal motive.

## Detecting Serious Mental Problems

The MMPI measures serious mental conditions such as neurosis and insanity, but most employers do not consider these to be personality characteristics. Rather, they are considered as medical disorders which require medical treatment. The MMPI measures these areas of insanity:

*Employees with serious mental condition can embarrass your company!*

## Schizophrenia scale

This scale measures traits such as being in-touch with reality, hallucinations, bizarre thoughts, and lack of impulse control. Scoring high on this scale may be cause for removal from consideration if the job duties would be impaired by this medical condition. Please note that many properly-medicated schizophrenics will not trigger this diagnosis.

## Psychopathic Deviate scale

This scale measures resistance to authority, lack of social mores and socially deviant behavior. Job applicants with this condition are rarely employable.

Remember that tests such as MMPI must be given by a trained psychologist, but the computer-generated report from the MMPI is often used when considering the right candidate for the job.

According to www.psychscreen.com, here is a sample from the verbal report section of an MMPI report:

*Mr. Sample is introverted and tends to be more comfortable when he is alone. An attachment deficit may exist as Mr. Sample describes engaging in significant avoidance and interpersonal withdrawal. Much social withdrawal exists as he actively avoids being with others.*

*A mild level of being over sensitive to and vigilant of others was described. Mr. Sample can blame others for his problems and generally sees the world as threatening and unfair. He expects others to be exceedingly untrustworthy, devious and act out for personal profit. He constantly expects others to lie, cheat, and manipulate to gain advantage.*

Now that we see the traits measured by the scientific tests, let's take a look at some other tests that are used to measure intelligence.

Numerous studies have shown that, Ceteris Paribas, intelligence is the single most important predictor of success at the job.

Because IQ is so important to job success, it is imperative that you use tools to evaluate the intelligence of each job candidate.

# Measuring Intelligence

Many hiring managers believe that hiring a smart person is the most important consideration and believe that intelligence is more important than job history, education or grades.

*Not all employees have equal intelligence.*

IBM Corporation has used this approach, and has a history of hiring smart graduates without any computer background. IBM believed that they could easily teach computer science to anyone with the intellect to learn quickly.

## Types of Intelligence

Most Psychologists recognize that there are several types of intelligence and your interview may include question that are designed to measure the candidates' cognitive ability.

Most experienced hiring managers can determine a candidates' intelligence during the interview since this is an area where it is difficult to fake a valid response. The specific types of intelligence we need to review include these:

- Linguistic intelligence
- Spatial Intelligence
- Kinesthetic Intelligence
- Interpersonal Intelligence
- Intrapersonal Intelligence
- Musical/Mathematical Intelligence

Let's take a look at intelligence-related job interview questions.

## Linguistic intelligence

Indicators of high linguistic intelligence include interest in reading, writing (including letters to the Editor) and doing word games and crossword puzzles. Interestingly, females tend to have higher scores in linguistic intelligence than males.

People with high linguistic intelligence are great communicators (although they may be poor public speakers) and excel at jobs like copyediting and book publishing.

## Spatial Intelligence

This measures the ability to think multi-dimensionally. High values are demonstrated in creativity and the ability to visualize complex problems in 3-dimensional space.

Jobs for high spatial-intelligence include pilots (map reading skills), engineering, computer analysts, and architects.

## Kinesthetic Intelligence

This type of intelligence measures coordination and the ability to have excellent muscle memory. Jobs requiring a high degree of this intelligence include athletics, carpentry, sewing, and mechanics.

## Interpersonal Intelligence

This measures a person's ability to empathize with others and work as a team member.

Often characterized by exceptional speaking skills, this type of intelligence is useful for jobs in management, counseling, teaching, and any job requiring a teamwork facilitator.

People with high interpersonal intelligence may not be suitable for jobs involving independent thinking and engineering.

## Intrapersonal Intelligence

This type of intelligence is evidenced by a self-motivated person who is good at independent thinking.

Jobs requiring high intrapersonal intelligence might include Psychologists, small-business owners, and entrepreneurs. Because they like to work independently, they tend to make poor team players and may not be suited for tasks involving teamwork.

## Musical/Mathematical Intelligence

This type of intelligence manifests itself in the ability to recognize patterns in music and numbers. People with high musical intelligence often make great mathematicians, actuaries, and computer programmers. Note that it is not necessary to have a background in music to have a high musical intelligence. People with high musical/mathematical intelligence enjoy well-structured tasks and solving complex problems.

This type of intelligence is beneficial for scientists, computer programmers, and jobs requiring logical reasoning. They are not well-suited to tasks involving creativity and out-of-the box thinking and make poor managers and inventors.

In studies on predictors of job performance, scientists conducted research into the factors that best predicted job performance. They considered cognitive test scores, biographical data, reference checks, education, interview results, college grades, and interest in the job in an effort to predict those metrics that would serve as the best predictor of job performance.

Intelligence tests have been around for nearly a century and the Stanford-Binet IQ exam was among the most popular. In the early 21$^{st}$ century there are IQ tests that do not require a psychologist, and many companies are using these paper-and-pencil measures of intellect to screen job candidates.

Popular paper-and-pencil IQ tests that you may be able to use include the list below. Remember, these tests have been administered millions of time and are very accurate:

- **Stanford-Binet Intelligence Scale** – The mother of all IQ tests. This must be given by a certified tester, normally a psychologist. The test covers four major areas including verbal reasoning, quantitative reasoning, abstract/visual reasoning, and short-term memory.

- **Slosson Full-Range Intelligence Test** – This is a 20 minute self-test that provides metrics related to intellectual abilities.

- **Kaufman Adolescent and Adult Intelligence Test** – This is a popular assessment exam, similar to the Stanford-Binet, and administered in less than one hour.

- **Cognitive Abilities Test** – This is a 3-hour comprehensive test to measure many areas of intelligence.

- **Raven's Progressive Matrices** – This is a 54-minute problem-solving test involving abstract design and special reasoning.

These intelligence tests have become required in many companies because they ensure that expensive training programs are not wasted on employees without the cognitive ability to complete the training. If it follows that the best predictor of job performance is intelligence, then what can you do to evaluate intellect during an interview?

The ability of smart people to excel at their job is well-documented. This is the reason that many companies recruit from top universities where the college admissions process has pre-screened applicants for intelligence.

 **Can I require an IQ test?**

Yes. Because so many companies are hiring solely based upon intellect, the Equal Employment Opportunity Commission (EEOC) has developed guidelines for the use of IQ testing. The intelligence test must be valid and fair, and the measure of intellect must only be a pert of the hiring process.

In the controversial best-seller *The Bell Curve*, the authors note that "the test score is a better predictor of job performance than any other single measure" (Figure 4.1).

---

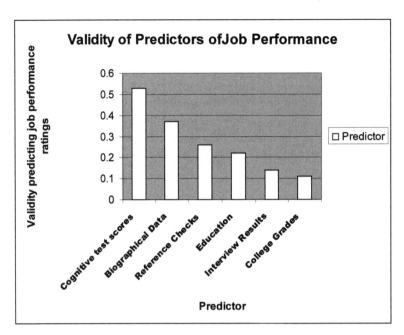

**Figure 4.1** – *Validity of job performance predictors (Hunter & Hunter, 1984)*

---

 **Can I infer a high IQ from a résumé?**

Many hiring managers can quickly spot smart candidates from their academic background. It is up to you to ensure that the candidate has the requisite brain cells to succeed at the job, and there are several valid ways to spot intelligent job candidates:

- **Deans List** - Make sure that you note those semesters where the candidate was included on the Deans List (GPA > 3.5) or the Chancellors list (GPA > 3.8).

- **SAT and ACT scores** – High College admission scores can go a long way toward helping validate intelligence. SAT scores above 1000 and ACT scores above 26 should be mentioned in a résumé. There are numerous studies that show a correlation between SAT scores and intellect (Willingham, 1962)

- **Academic Fraternities** – Phi Beta Kappa and other academic Greek organization membership indicate high cognitive skills.

- **Honors** – The National Junior Honor Society (High School) and National Honor Society (College) helps to verify intelligence. In addition, take special note if the candidate has graduated Summa Cum Laude, Magna Cum Laude, or Cum Laude.

Below we see the results of a 1962 study plotting the correlation of Otis IQ scores and SAT scores. While it is very difficult to use the SAT as an absolute predictor of intelligence (because kids of many different ages take the test), it is considered by some to be a fairly accurate predictor of intelligence. (Figure 4.2)

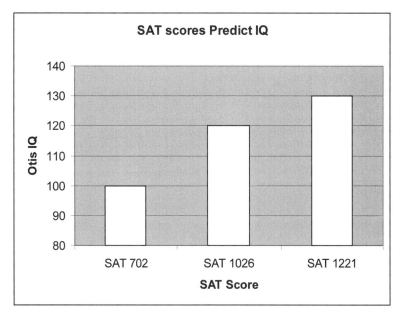

**Figure 4.2** – *Correlation between IQ and SAT scores (Willingham, 1962)*

As we can see, there are many unobtrusive yet reliable indicators of intelligence.

However, there are also "red flag" items that indicate a candidate is falsely trying to appear intelligent. Let's take a closer look at these candidate killers.

---

### ☠ Discount Phony IQ Indicators

---

Here we will discuss some problematic intelligence-related résumé items. Many managers will immediately remove any résumé that contains these red-flag intelligence items.

Candidates with purchased honors, at-home certifications, or scientifically-invalid measures of intelligence on their résumé rarely make successful employees. The rule-of-thumb is to eliminate any candidate who included honors that require some payment or a paid inclusion in a book listing scholars. Some red-flag résumé items might include:

- **High IQ societies** – Some IQ tests are not considered scientifically valid by many psychologists, and candidates who put memberships in a High-IQ society membership on a résumé may have low feelings of self-worth.

- **Purchased Honors** – Many organizations offer paid inclusion prestige books that make it look like the candidate has some significant intellectual achievement. You should carefully check and ensure that candidates with bogus honors are not given an opportunity to interview.

- **Phony College Degrees** – These rarely get past the HR department and they are a sure-sign of either low self-esteem or fraudulent intentions. Some of these diploma mills allow

---

you to buy a high GPA, and almost all HR departments will verify your degree.

# Job Questions to measure Intelligence

There are several unobtrusive measures that will let you know about the intellectual abilities of any job candidate.

William Shockley, the Nobel Laureate and writer, was noted for his job interviews where he would access the creative intelligence of candidates by asking them open-ended questions, specially designed to measure intellect. This approach has been adopted by thousands of companies, each of whom devises their own open-ended problem solving questions.

William Poundstone, the author of "*How Would You Move Mount Fuji?: Microsoft's Cult of the Puzzle — How the World's Smartest Companies Select the Most Creative Thinkers,*" describes how to pose problem-solving question to job applicants and time their responses with a stopwatch.

In the following pages you will find some of my favorite intelligence questions. While not scientific they provide me with a gage of the cognitive ability of a job candidate.

---

**?**   **How would you estimate the number of Book Stores in New York State?**

---

This question is designed to measure the candidates' ability to solve problems when not all the data is known. (By the way, you can quite accurately estimate this number if you know how to analyze the problem).

---

The best answer would include a procedure to gather a statistically-meaningful sample and then generalize it to the whole population.

*I would start with online phone books and Neilsen demographic data.*

*I would count the number of bookstores in several sample areas, rural, suburban and urban, and extrapolate the density of bookstores for each population area.*

*I would then generalize the sample by getting the total population of New York Sate and the percentage of the population in rural, suburban and urban areas.*

*I could then generalize the sample to the total population.*

**?  What magazines and newspapers do you subscribe to, and why do you like them?**

This question can measure the linguistic intelligence of the job candidate. Good answers would include any periodicals that tend to be read by smart people.

It is amazing how many candidates give a false answer to this question, trying to impress you and not realizing that you may read the same periodicals.  Of course, the candidates are always unable to answer specific questions about articles.

Best answers include periodicals that are read by populations with a higher IQ.

These might include Newsweek, Time, US News & World Report, The New Yorker, Wall Street Journal, and so on.

As for the second part to the question, *"Why do you like these periodicals?"* Almost any answer is acceptable so long as it sites specific qualities of the periodical.

**? Tell me about the books that have you read in the past six months?**

This is an excellent indicator of IQ as numerous studies (and common sense) show that intelligent people tend to read more than less intelligent candidates.

 **Top Answer**

The best answer to this question involves diversity. You do not want candidates who respond that they only read technical manuals. You are seeking candidates with a wide range of interests.

While enjoyment of reading is not a scientific indicator of IQ it can give you an idea about the diversity of interests and the candidates' personality.

While decorum prevents me from listing those authors who tend to have a blue-collar audience, there are many mainstream authors whose audience consists of readers with IQ scores over 110.

Candidates may respond that they enjoy a wide range of topics including non-fiction, history, biographies or novels.

# Preparing for the Interview

## Learn about the Company

Once each candidate has passed your résumé screening and background checks, you are ready for the on-site interview. Your job during the job interview is to locate the best candidate for the job, the one who possess the correct technical and interpersonal skills to excel at the job duties.

Just as you have carefully reviewed the résumé and work history of the candidate, you should expect the successful candidate to demonstrate knowledge of your company, its products, history, and management.

Remember, you should always ask the question *"Why do you want to work HERE?"*, and this will be the candidates' opportunity to show that they have researched your company and understand the main business and economic issues.

Failing to learn about an employer could very well be the kiss-of-death for the candidate. Many employers believe that a candidate may as well not bother showing-up for an interview without detailed knowledge of the company in their back-pocket. Any good job candidate will usually have performed the following tasks:

- Visited your company web site
- Checked Google News and Google Groups
- Find industry reviews about your company

- Evaluated the economic status of your company

- Done a keyword search on Google

 **How will a candidate find-out about my company?**

The answer is right at their fingertips, using the Google search engine. The appearance of the companies' web site can tell a lot about the way the company is managed. A professional web site with custom graphics and frequent content update indicates a forward-thinking company.

Does your web site have a section for press releases? If so, ask questions to make sure that the candidate has read them.

Does your web site have a link to a text-only version of the site? Do all of your graphics have a test description of the image? If so, this indicates that you comply with the *Americans with Disabilities Act* and are friendly to the disabled.

Does your web site contain biographical information about your top management? This indicates that your company is proud of the quality of its staff and gives you an opportunity to see if the candidate is motivated enough to read about the management.

If there are biographical pages, the savvy candidate will read them carefully, paying special note to those management qualities that are highlighted. For example, if the management biographies emphasize the innovative talents of management, then it is highly likely that the candidate will emphasize their personal innovation.

To completely research your company, a few well-placed Google searches will reveal volumes of information. Let's take a look at how your winning candidate can quickly gather the information needed to answer several of your important interview questions, most importantly the guaranteed question *"Why do you want to work HERE?"*

## Do a keyword search on Google

Google is an amazing resource and a few well-placed Google searches may reveal forums and message boards that discuss your company in detail. For example, to see what people are saying about Waldo Widgets, we could enter the following searches. Note that the double-quotes ensure word proximity and provide better precision and recall for your Google search (Figure 5.1).

"waldo widgets"
"waldo widgets" employee
"waldo widgets" lawsuit
"waldo widgets" sucks

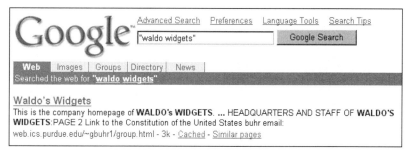

**Figure 5.1** – *A sample Google Search*

Once a web search is completed, they might also check Google News and Google Groups. These resources will often provide additional information about your company.

To make it easy to find news and group discussions, Google provides search tabs affording the ability to quickly re-issue a web search against Google News or Google Groups (Figure 5.2).

**Figure 5.2 –** *The Google Groups and Google News tabs*

Once the News and Groups tabs are found, just click the tab to re-issue the query against the News database. Below is an example where the search term was "IBM", and the Google News button was clicked (Figure 5.3)

**Figure 5.3 –** *A Google News Search for IBM*

A listing of the current new stories about IBM will be shown. Any candidate who really wants the job will have read these articles so you can confidently ask applicants about the recent new on your company.

For more detailed information about what people are saying about your company, try Google Groups (Figure 5.4).

Google Groups is an online version of the popular Usenet newsgroups that have been available for more than a decade. They contain archives of millions of messages and allow anyone to view comments about your company.

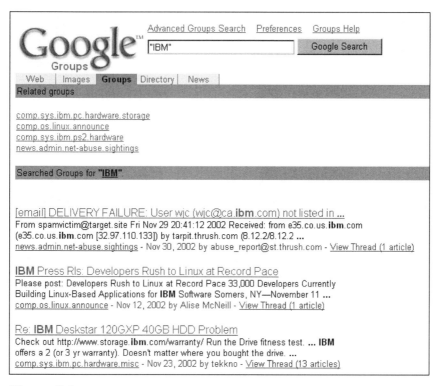

**Figure 5.4 –** *Google Groups for IBM*

Of course, many posts in Google Groups are anonymous and are never regarded as the Gospel truth.

However, many anonymous postings to Google groups are from prior employees who want to vent, so this can be a tremendous resource for the savvy job candidate to find out what people are really saying about your company.

> **What other tools will a candidate use to research my company?**

For publicly-traded Corporations, checking the Yahoo message boards is a great way to understand the climate surrounding the company. These message boards are totally un-moderated and anonymous, making them a perfect place to see what employees and stockholders are thinking (Figure 5.5).

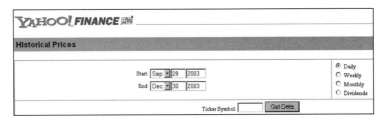

**Figure 5.5 –** *Yahoo Financials stock symbol query screen*

The stock prices and a link to "messages" are keyed by the company stock ticker symbol. Here your savvy candidate can find un-censored comments about your company (Figure 5.6).

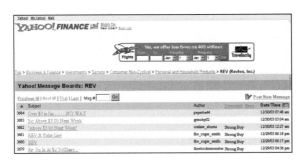

**Figure 5.6 –** *Yahoo Message Board comments*

## How will a candidate read newspaper stories about my company?

For a candidate to find recent reports about your company, they just click the "sort by date" link on the far right-hand side of the Google result screen. This will show the most recent Google Groups or Google News listing first in the result set (Figure 5.7)

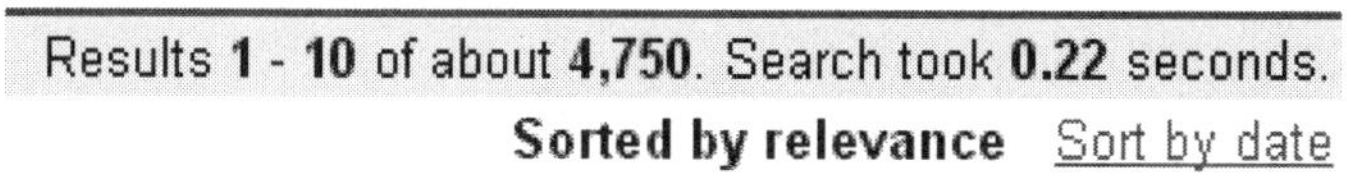
Results 1 - 10 of about 4,750. Search took 0.22 seconds.
Sorted by relevance Sort by date

**Figure 5.7 –** *The sort by date option*

This option show all Google news reports sorted in reverse chronological order. The savvy job candidate will have read all of these stories because they know that the person who gets the job offer will be the one who has taken the time to show they understand what's happening inside your company.

Of course, you should also re-read these article and take copious note so that you will be able to ask pointed questions during the interview.

# The Telephone Interview

## CHAPTER 6

## Telephone Pre-screening

Before investing the time to have a candidate on-site, a telephone pre-screening should be conducted to quickly eliminate inappropriate candidates.

*The telephone is your best tool for pre-screening candidates.*

---

The initial phone contact is a basic check of communication skills. You want a candidate that sounds bright, articulate, and has a pleasant accent-neutral tone.

The quality of diction is especially important for jobs requiring contact with outside clients or customers. The successful job candidate has no detectable accent, (especially for jobs requiring external contact with customers) clear enunciation, and correct grammar.

There are usually two distinct telephone interviews:

**Tech-Check** – This is an assessment and verification that the candidate possesses the skills required to perform the job. This is normally performed by your senior technical person and consists of unambiguous technical questions.

**Management Interview** – This is your opportunity to access the candidate at a deeper level and see if they are likely to be a good fit for the organization.

Using the details from previous chapters you should be able to formulate the critical questions and quickly weed-out the uninterested candidate and focus your attention on the candidates who have done their pre-interview homework.

## The telephone tech-check interview

Prior to asking a job candidate on-site you may ask a candidate to participate in a technical interview to access whether their skill sets meet the job requirements.

This interview is usually done by the companies' top technical person and the interview is highly structured with pointed "correct answer" questions.

For example, a candidate interviewing for a computer support position might be asked *"Where would you find the registry parameters that control MS-Word?*

Of course, these questions have only one correct answer and the technical interview is an absolute prerequisite in most companies.

For details, see Appendix B where you will find a tech-check list of common technical questions for measuring office computer skills.

Examples of question for the telephone tech-check for a clerical position might include right-wrong questions designed to verify skills. For a complete list see Appendix B, but here are a couple of examples:

*Name some common anti-virus products*

*How does Rich Text Format (.rtf) differ from a MS-Word document?*

*How do you create a blind distribution list in MS-Outlook?*

This initial technical interview may screen-out more than 50% of your short-list candidates. A well-executed telephone interview should be concise, to-the-point, and allow you to get critical information about the suitability of the candidate.

Next let's look at a checklist of telephone interview questions.

## Telephone Interview Checklist

The following pages provide some of the top telephone interview questions and the most common answers. This all-important pre-screening can quickly narrow-down your search and ensure that you do not waste your precious time talking with inappropriate job candidates.

- Why do you want to work here?

- What are your wage requirements?

- Why do you want to leave your present job?

- What do you like least about your existing job?

- Tell me about your most significant accomplishment?

- What is your greatest shortcoming?

- Why are you the ideal person for this job?

- Have you ever been fired or been in-trouble with the law?

- Are you willing to work evenings and weekends?

Using this checklist you can quickly pre-screen a multitude of job candidates. Again, this is a pre-screening interview and if the candidate answers these questions to your satisfaction you can proceed to schedule the on-site interview.

## ? Why do you want to work HERE?

Here is the candidate's chance to shine and show that they are sincerely interested in working for your company. The best responses would include information related to the size of your company, the market status, and the quality of your management.

This is an important question because you want to know if they have singled-out your company, or if they are simply desperate for any job.

Some of the best candidates will have research the background of all top management and will state specific reasons why they want to work for your company, citing specific achievements. In the best cases, the candidate will mention your own personal background and show knowledge of your specific qualities and skills. Sample answers might include:

*I've always wanted to work for a company that has been rated one of the top 500 places to work in the USA.*

*I really want to work for your company because I would get a change to work with a Mr. Jones the Nobel Laureate.*

*I like your company because of your astonishing track record in out-performing your competition three years in a row.*

*I have heard some very good things about your company and I think that I would be an excellent fit.*

## ? What are your wage requirements?

This is a make-or-break question and you should never schedule an on-site interview with any candidate who has unrealistic compensation requirements.

The savvy candidate is realistic, yet conservative in their wage needs and knows that if they are hired and contribute to the company their salary will be adjusted according to their real value.

**Top Answer**

Many job candidates are taken-aback with this abrupt question and often react with a vague response like *"Whatever you think I'm worth"*.

This is an extremely poor answer because any worthwhile job candidate knows approximately what their skills are worth in the current market. Top answers would include:

*I need at least $70,000, but I expect that you will find me to be worth far more than that.*

*I'm currently earning $45,000 and I feel that I'm undervalued.*

**?** **Why do you want to leave your present job?**

The best answer here is lack of challenge or lack of opportunity for advancement.

Remember, this is a critical question for you because you are prohibited from contacting their current employer. This is your attempt to ascertain the candidates' real motive for changing jobs.

 **Hidden Agenda: Is the candidate in jeopardy of being fired? Do they harbor resentment towards their employer? Are they a troublemaker or poor performer?**

This open-ended question may alert you to problems in the candidate's workplace including poor work history or problems working with co-workers.

The best candidates will never bash their current employer, even if they have resentment. Instead, they will cite issues surrounding the job duties and challenges of their existing job. Top answers include:

The savvy candidate will answer all questions with a positive spin, even those questions that are negative by nature.

They will resist the temptation to mention their overbearing boss or the poor treatment at their present job. A good answer to this question should focus on limitations of the job and career opportunities, and never focus on personalities.

Some of the best answers include:

**Boredom** - *I have mastered my work and it is not challenging enough for me anymore.*

**No challenge** - *I am capable of doing far more complex work, but there are no openings.*

**No advancement** – *My current company is privately-owned and the children of the owner are being groomed to fill all top positions.*

**?**   **What do you like least about your existing job?**

This gives the candidate an opportunity to vent and say bad things about their job, boss and co-workers.

---

**Hidden Agenda: Is this candidate a whiney person? Do they have trouble working with others?**

It is surprising how many candidates seize upon this opportunity to say extremely hurtful things about co-workers and management. This is a sure-fire red-flag, and these candidates rarely get to the on-site interview.

 **Top Answer**

The savvy candidate knows never to mention anything relating to personalities of management, even if it is true. Instead, the job candidate should cite tangible issues with their job. Best answers include:

*I have a new baby at home and I cannot work weekends anymore.*

*I want a job with a shorter commute.*

*My company is relocating to Botswana and I want to stay in this area.*

**?    Tell me about your most significant accomplishment.**

This is the candidates' chance to shine and describe how they might be beneficial to you. Be careful not to phrase the question as "work-related" accomplishment in order to see if the candidate wants to mention non-work-related achievements.

---

Telephone Pre-screening

**Top Answer**

The best answer should include both the tangible and intangible benefits of their previous work and the answer does not necessarily have to be work-related. Sample top answers might include:

*I saved over two million dollars with my automation idea.*

*I increased customer satisfaction by 30% leading to improved sales.*

*My marketing promotion was so successful that it is still being used today.*

*My invention was considered so important that it was patented.*

*I saved a child from downing last year.*

**?** **What is your greatest shortcoming?**

This is an almost universal job question and one that they must be very careful when answering. This is a tricky question and often takes the candidate off-guard. Candidates may think silently for a period, while other may reply with a flippant remark like *"I'm perfect"*. A funny or flippant answer to this question is a major red-flag because they fail to appreciate the serious nature of the question.

 **Top Answer**

The question is posed to allow the candidate to show self-awareness and insight into their interpersonal and work habits. A good answer to this question should focus on knowledge-based weaknesses (e.g. *"I want to learn statistics"*) and human-skills areas (e.g. *"I want to improve my problem-solving skills"*). The best answers might include:

*I need to improve my analytical skills and I'm taking a Calculus class.*

*I tend to be too goal-oriented and I sometimes have trouble stepping-back from an important project.*

*I tend to become impatient with lazy co-workers*

*I have low tolerance for laziness and stupidity*

*I get impatient when a co-worker impedes my progress on a project.*

---

**?    Why are you the ideal person for this job?**

---

This is the candidate's opportunity to emphasize those skills and personality traits that will lend the most value to the company bottom-line.

Responses such as *"I don't know"*, or *"I don't know what you are looking for:"* and clear red-flags as it indicates that the applicant has not taken the time to research the position.

---

    **Top Answer**

---

They should be realistic and not out-of-sync with their academic and work history yet emphasize those aspects of their history that are spot-on with the job description.

---

Top answer might include:

*I have the exact training and experience background for the job, plus I'm highly motivated to take-on more responsibility.*

*I have a degree from the same school as your top department manager, so I think that I will have the skills to perform as well as he does.*

*What I lack in experience I make-up for in drive and ambition. I'm willing to learn skills on my own-time and I have no problem putting-in long work hours to make certain that I succeed.*

> **?** **Are you willing to work evenings and weekends?**

This is a very critical question. You need to know, right from the outset whether the candidate places outside interests above their job duties.

This is an especially important question if it is a salaried job and you expect the candidate to regularly work more than 40 hours per week.

Candidates with religious or family obligations might not be appropriate for a job that requires long-hours and evening or holiday work.

>  **Top Answer**

The top answer should indicate that the candidate is willing to work whenever needed, even if they have restrictions.

Top answers might include:

---

*I have obligation most weekends, but I can re-schedule them if I know about the issue in-advance.*

*I have no family or life outside my job. In my last job I often slept in the office when things got crazy.*

---

**? Have you ever been in trouble with the law?**

This question is deliberately phrased to require the job candidate to mention all arrests and convictions, even if they were misdemeanor parking violations.

---

**Hidden Agenda: Is the candidate lying about embarrassing incidents?**

The knowledgeable job candidate knows that all arrest and criminal convictions are a matter of public record (and available within 5 minutes on the Internet), so this question is not always a measure of honesty.

The dishonesty from lying about their history is often a larger red-flag than the criminal offense. Remember, employers cannot discriminate because of an arrest record.

---

 **Top Answer**

Here, you must measure the severity of the moral turpitude against their candor for admitting their shortcomings. Top answers include:

---

*I was charged and arrested based on a false accusation, but they convicted the real perpetrator and exonerated me of all charges.*

# The On-site Interview     CHAPTER 7

## Conducting the On-site Interview

As a brief review, there are several types of interviews:

- The initial telephone interview
- The telephone tech-check interview
- Your telephone interview
- The on-site HR interview
- Your on-site manager interview
- The on-site team interview

Now we are ready to conduct the most detailed of all, the on-site interview.

Once your short-list candidates have successfully passed their telephone interviews you will invite each candidate to appear on-site for a personal interview.

Some companies conduct interviews with several key employees including the Human Resources Manager, you, and your team.

The on-site interview is usually the last step before extending a job offer, so this is your final opportunity to evaluate each candidate.  Let's take a closer look at each phase.

## The on-site HR interview

Once the candidate has passed the technical evaluation its time for a face-to-face interview.  In many companies your first point of contact is with the HR manager. The HR manager probably has the most experience of all interviewers because it is their job to interview all job candidates for the entire company. You could consider them experts at devising questions that relate to personality and suitability for the job.

As most HR personnel can attest, after several thousand interviews they develop a "radar" that allows them to quickly size-up a job candidate. Hence, as a hiring manager, you should value and weigh the HR person's input appropriately when making your final decision.

## Your on-site manager interview

As the hiring manager, you are the person who will spend the most time with the candidate. You will normally be the candidate's direct supervisor, and this is your only chance to make sure that you hire the best person for the job.

Your interview is the most important of all of the on-site interviews because you may have veto authority over the HR manager and your team members.

## The on-site team interview

This is the final stage in most on-site interviews. It provides the staff a change to talk with the candidate. Sometimes the team interview takes place in a restaurant or bar so that the team can access how well the candidate will fit into the organization.

Remember, while the hiring manager makes the recommendation for hire, the staff and HR manager have tremendous influence in their decision.

During your on-site interview you will judge the candidate along several dimensions. You judge the candidate for their personality, intelligence, their understanding of company culture, table manners and a host of other factors. By this point, their technical skills will have been accessed, and the main purpose of your on-site interview is to ensure that they are "right" for your company. Let's look at some common manager questions about the on-site interview.

*"My long-term career goal?*
*Actually, I want to get your job."*

The candidate's knowledge of the corporate culture is very important. They should have done research and ensured that they are dressed appropriately for the workplace. A good candidate will always ask about appropriate dress if they cannot ascertain this information from Google. Failure to dress appropriately can be cause for immediate termination of the interview if the organization has a dress code.

*Don't be forced to reprimand an employee for improper dress.*

Some companies publish their dress code. For example, in the 1960s through the 1980's IBM male employees were required to wear blue pinstripe suits, while shirts, maroon ties, and black wingtip shoes. No exceptions.

Formal institutions (Banks, Attorneys) have a strict dress code. For example, I have seen candidates sent home immediately if they are wearing a sports coat, a non-white shirt, a loud tie, non-dress shoes, etc. I have also seen job applicants mocked behind their backs for wearing an off-the-rack brown or dark green suit to an interview.

If the candidate is interviewing for a management position (Manager, Director, Vice President), then they must wear an expensive suit that is custom tailored. Someone who works around executives all day can recognize a cheap $400 suit at 50 paces, and they can just as easily recognize a fine $3,000 Italian suit.

*Proper job interview attire is important.*

Well-mannered employees are always highly-prized. Candidates should be judged for appropriate behavior, etiquette and demeanor at all times. Common etiquette issues include:

**Poor Eye Contact** – The candidate should always make direct eye contact at all times. Poor eye contact indicates low self-esteem and is considered rude in many cases.

**Dead-fish handshake** – A cold, clammy, sweaty, and limp handshake is a major turn-off. You should always wipe you hands unobtrusively before shaking hands, and your grip should be firm, without squeezing too hard. A handshake should always be accompanied by dead-on eye contact.

**Understand Pecking Order** – Many job applicants are not aware that they should stand on the left of a superior (the position of honor is on the right), and when entering a vehicle, enter before their superior.

**Dining Etiquette** – It is astonishing how many job applicants are excluded because of poor table manners.

*Good manners are critical for group-work environments!*

Now that we know the basics, let's take a look at the common "interview killers," statements and behaviors that most managers consider just-cause for immediate rejection.

*Wonder why you never get that second interview?*

 **Know the interview killers.**

There are several practices that are red-flags and sure-fire indicators that the candidate is not right for your company.

Many managers immediately discard interview candidates that have the following characteristics.

**Non-specific about career goals –** The ideal job candidate has a tight focus and indicates that they are interested in a very specific job position. Avoid candidates who make statements like *"I would be willing to consider any position that you have available"*.

**Repeatedly mentions personal values –** For example, the candidate who repeatedly mentions how trustworthy they are is usually untrustworthy, else they would not be making such a big deal about it.

**Excessive personal chatter –** While the candidate may have some interesting outside activities, hobbies, and interests, they should keep the focus on work-related skills. Too much discussion of non-work activities is a red-flag and calls into question their dedication to their career.

> ☠ **Interpersonal conflict and problems with management.**

These are red flags and will immediately make a manager wonder about the suitability of the candidates' personality.

**Unfair treatment –** Look out for comments like *"I was wrongfully written-up for poor work productivity."*

**Poor People skills –** Be alert for any statements that make it appear as if the candidate is hard to get along with, such as *"My co-workers are jerks and they are always sabotaging my work."*

**Bad Management –** We know that some employees will resent management, regardless of their treatment. Be alert for red-flag statements like *"My boss is a tyrant and is constantly hounding me to improve."*

Next, let's take a look at questions that are illegal or inappropriate for you to ask at an interview. This does not mean that you don't need to know this information, only that you may be prohibited by law from asking about certain information or considering it in your hiring decision.

# Illegal Interview Questions

## What Not to Ask

There are many questions that you cannot ask, either on the written job application or during an oral interview. These include questions regarding age, race, disabilities, religion, national origin, or gender.

Of course, the answers to many of these questions will be easily answered with a routine background check. Let's take a look at these illegal questions and techniques for legally getting this information.

*Don't wind-up in court over an illegal interview question!*

# Age

Age-based job discrimination is against the law, but asking the candidate's date of birth is not illegal. The *Equal Employment Opportunity Commission* (EEOC) and the *Age Discrimination in Employment Act of 1967* does not prohibit a prospective employer from asking your date of birth.

*Age discrimination can be costly!*

However, if age is a direct factor is the person's ability to perform the job, you may be able to make it part of the criteria for making your hiring decision, for example:

**Airline Pilots** – The FAA requires that all pilots be retired at age 60.

**Models** – Modeling agencies may specify people of certain age groups for modeling age-appropriate clothing.

---

**Machine Operators** – Regardless of disabilities, jobs that require a low probability of traumatic loss of consciousness may deny employment solely on the basis of age. For example, an octogenarian may have a 70% probability of a Myocardial Infraction (heart attack) that would prevent them from safely operating dangerous equipment.

Of course, you will probably know the candidate's approximate age from their résumé, and it is extremely difficult for any candidate to win an age discrimination lawsuit unless your company shows a well-documented pattern of discriminatory practices.

## Racial background

Surprisingly, the candidate's race may be considered as a factor for companies that promote "diversity" in the workplace. While you may not directly ask about ethnicity, rest assured that you will be able to glean this information from their résumé and background check.

## Religion

Like it or not, for some employers the candidate's religion may play an important role in the hiring decision. If a candidates religious beliefs mandate prolonged absences from work, or missing certain critical work times, then you may want to know this information.

Surprisingly, knowledge of a candidate's religion can also work in their favor. For example, computer shops commonly perform maintenance during Christian holidays and non-Christian employees are ideal for this work. Also, employers in small communities many consider how well the job candidate will fit-in to the community, especially if the job is located in a small rural area.

Other religious discrimination may be allowed. For example a member of the Scik religion may not be able to dress appropriately for a financial institution that requires clean-shaven employees. In rejecting these applicants, the presence of facial hair (not the religion) may be cited as reason for refusal to hire.

Smart employers may be able to obtain the candidates religious background with a routine background check or from the candidates' résumé, especially if the candidate provides church-related items on their résumé.

## National Origin

While it is illegal to discriminate on the basis of national origin, US employers are required to have the job candidate provide proof that they are eligible to work in the USA. Of course, the candidate's national origin can also be gleaned from work visas and educational records.

## Disabilities

The Americans with Disabilities Act prohibits discrimination on the basis of physical disabilities unless the disability absolutely prevents the person from performing the job duties. For example, a paraplegic may be disqualified from working on a loading dock.

However, the issue gets very tricky when the disability does not prevent the person from perform the job, although hiring them might cost your company thousands of dollars. For example, all computer systems must be fully accessible for employees who use them, and the introduction of a visually impaired employee may force the re-design of a multi-million dollar system, just to accommodate one employee.

*Some disabilities can affect work performance.*

## Illegal vs. Inappropriate Questions

We must distinguish between interview questions that are illegal versus those that are inappropriate. This is an important distinction because you cannot ask any interview questions that violate the law.

## Disability & Medical Questions

Outages relating to medical issues result in the loss of billions of dollars per year in productivity and employers are always cognizant of those potential losses, especially for salaried employees.

Companies that fund their own medical insurance plans are also super-sensitive to medical issues because a single sick employee could drain millions of dollars from the fund.

Let's take a look at some loaded questions and examine the legal ways to ask them at an interview.

> **?**     **May we contact your current employer?**

This is a loaded (but legal) question. Surely, the candidate does not want their current employer to know that they are leaving their job, yet they want to appease the interviewer.

Many job candidates consider this to be an extremely unprofessional question and may terminate the interview!

> **?**     **Do you have any disability that might prevent you from performing your job duties?**

This is a perfectly legal and legitimate question and they must answer truthfully.

## Criminal history

The rules on considering criminal history vary by the type of job. Employers in law enforcement may ask candidates if they have ever been arrested or charged with a crime, either felony or misdemeanor.

Other employers may only ask if they have been convicted of a crime when using a disclaimer that their answer will not necessarily disqualify them for the job.

> **?**  **Have you ever been convicted of any crimes other than misdemeanor traffic violations?**

This is valid legal question and one that an applicant must answer truthfully because any conviction history will appear on the background check. The only exceptions to this are convictions that occurred while the candidate was a minor (sealed records).

> **?**  **Have you ever been in trouble with the law?**

This is also a legal question and deliberately vague in order to illicit the most information from the candidate.

However, ask these questions inappropriately and you could find yourself in a lawsuit.

> **?**  **Have you ever been arrested?**

You are not allowed to ask this question because all people are presumed innocent until convicted. When faced with this question, the job candidate faces a dilemma because the arrest record will appear in their background check, and lying might be cause for removal from consideration.

## Parental Status

A major loss of productivity for a company is employees with small children. When an employee becomes a new parent, the "Family Leave" Act allows a parent to take a non-paid furlough with guaranteed re-hire, regardless of the ramifications to the employer.

Hence, employers are very interested in knowing the answers to questions relating to their long-term work availability.

However, you must be very careful when broaching the subject, even in casual conversation, lest the candidate suspect that you might use the information as a factor in the hiring decision.

**? Do you plan on starting a family?**

This question might come-up during casual conversation, and here the candidate must dance a fine-line between appearing forthright versus being perceived as evasive.

**? Are you pregnant?**

This question may be very important to you, particularly in-light of the requirements of the Family Medical Leave Act. Of course, it is none of your business, and the candidate cannot be held accountable for lying in the case of this inappropriate question.

**? I have here toddlers at home. Do you have small children?**

Asking questions like these are not only inappropriate, but may also be illegal. However, because of their importance to some employers, a simple background check and a review of records will disclose the ages of their children without exposing you to a potential lawsuit.

## Marital Status

It is believed by some employers that married executives are more successful at their duties than unmarried executives. Also, some medical research suggests that unmarried people suffer from more illness-related downtime and stress than their married counterparts.

This is delicate question and it can only be broached during casual conversation.

> **?** **My wife loves to ride horses. What does you wife like to do?**

Remember, you may be prohibited by law from considering this information as part of your hiring decision.

As we can see, you will have many ulterior motives and hidden agendas, all relating to your fear of potential loss of work time. Some employers feel strongly about getting the answers to these questions but are very careful to ask these questions in an innocent way and not to document these issues in writing.

# How to handle an offended Candidate

To fully understand how a job candidate handles stress, you may have an opportunity to bring-up embarrassing issues and watch the candidate dance-around embarrassing questions.

These embarrassing areas might include unexplained gaps in work history. If the candidate has a less-than stellar work history, they may be forced to explain the situation during their interview.

The savvy candidate knows that you have carefully scanned their résumé to find unexplained gaps in employment. They know that they cannot "fudge" their résumé about employment dates because almost all HR departments will confirm their actual dates of employment.

For some sensitive jobs, the candidate may be required to sign a "Release of Information" form, giving their prospective employer access to confidential Medical, Educational, and Personnel files.

Remember, it is extremely difficult for a job candidate to successfully sue you for considering illegal and inappropriate information in your hiring decision. Even if they file a lawsuit and win, the damage amount will seldom outweigh the legal expenses.

If you decide to ask an inappropriate or illegal question, the candidate has an immediate decision to make. They can just pleasantly answer the question, refuse to answer the question, or gerrymander around the question.

Remember, the candidate must now ascertain whether your question was innocent or malicious. For example, during an interview lunch, it's not uncommon to discuss personal interests and hobbies. The candidate has three choices, a direct answer, refusal to answer, or to raise hell.

## Refuse to answer

The job candidate has the absolute right to refuse to answer any question, and if they feel that the illegal question was not malicious they may politely point-out that the question is inappropriate.

## Raise Hell

On the other hand, if the candidate feels that you are being grossly unprofessional or malicious, then they may decide to chuck the job, and get the satisfaction of a loud tirade about all of the trouble that they will make for you for attempting to use discriminatory hiring practices.

Of course, this action will generally exclude them from further consideration for the job, so make sure that they understand the ramifications of challenging the motive behind an inappropriate question.

Next we get right to the heart of this book and examine the top on-site job interview questions, their hidden agendas and the top answers for each question.

# The Top On-Site Interview Questions

## Universal Questions

The following job interview questions are almost universal and they can expect to discuss these issues during their interview.

- What are your long-term career goals?

- I need somebody quickly. If you are selected, when could you start?

- Can we contact your previous employers?

- Tell me about a time when you helped improve an employee's poor work performance?

- How would you compare your verbal skills to your writing skills?

- Tell me about how you have handled an unsatisfied customer?

- What is the description for your ideal job?

- What questions do you have?

Let's take a closer look at these questions and their top answers.

> **?**    **What are your long-term career goals?**

Here we are looking for evidence that the job candidate takes their career seriously and has developed a well-reasoned and realistic career plan.

Remember, you will have the candidates' résumé in-hand, so they should never express a grandiose plan that is not reflected in their work and academic history.

The best job candidate will have a realistic career goal, in-line with their education and circumstances. For example, it might be unrealistic to hear a 35 year-old high school drop-out with 4 small children at home talk about achieving an executive management position, while this might not be unrealistic for a 26 year-old MBA. The best answers might include:

*I want to push myself to the limit, and I'm finishing Graduate School on evenings and weekends*

*I'm taking Internet-based training to improve my accounting skills and I hope to become a CPA someday.*

*I'm always trying to improve myself and I don't mind working extra hours to learn a new job skill.*

**?** **I need somebody right away. If you are selected, when would you be able to start?**

This question should be asked with a sense of urgency, making the candidate feel as if they might not get the job unless they "screw" their existing employer by walking-out without notice.

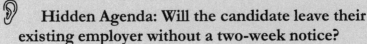 **Hidden Agenda: Will the candidate leave their existing employer without a two-week notice?**

This question will measure the candidate's sense of obligation. If the candidate is willing to walk-out of their existing job without notice, they will probably do the same to you someday.

 **Top Answer**

Regardless of your implied sense of urgency, the employee should say that it would be unfair to just walk-out on their existing boss and that they feel obligated to give two-weeks notice.

**?** **May we contact your previous employer?**

This is a loaded question especially if the candidate believes that their previous employer may not give a glowing recommendation.

In almost all large companies, the Human Resources person is directed only to confirm their job title and dates of employment, and nothing else, so they may be safe.

Remember, you may not need the candidate's permission to contact their previous employer, and this can be damaging if you can bypass the HR department and speak directly with their supervisor.

In smaller companies however, the manager-to-manager relationship may be fatal. For example, many managers know that they cannot sue for off-the-record comments and personal opinions.

For example, instead of saying "Joe did not perform his job well", the manager could simply say "I would not hire him," thereby making it impossible for them to pursue any litigation.

> **?**   **Tell me about a time when you helped improve an employee's poor work performance?**

This open-ended question gives the candidate a chance to articulate their social and analytical skills.

>    **Top Answer**

Because the question deals with the possible hurt feelings of the poor performer, this is a great way to access the tact and finesse of the candidate.  Top answers might include:

*I pointed-out the problem in an unemotional and non-threatening way, without attributing any blame to the worker.  We then worked together to devise a solution to the performance problem.*

*I was especially careful not to hurt their feelings but I was very clear that there was a deficiency that had to be corrected.*

*I tried to work with the person to get to the root of the problem and made them feel safe that I was not going to report the poor performance to management.*

> **?**   **How would you compare your verbal skills to your writing skills?**

---

This question reveals the candidate's subjective judgment of their communications skills.

Of course, the candidate's résumé provides clues into their writing skills, and their oral skills can be inferred by participation on debating teams, college communications courses, and membership in Toastmasters.

 **Hidden Agenda: How self-aware is the candidate about their personal deficiencies?**

Can the candidate comfortably discuss their own shortcomings, or are they the type of person who blames everything on others?

 **Top Answer**

Most people will say that their verbal skills need the most work, but there is no correct answer to this question.

Instead, the purpose of this question is to see if the candidate is forthcoming about the deficiencies and willing to take corrective action.

Best answers might include accurate descriptions of their issues and insights into the proper corrective actions.

**?** **Tell me about how you have handled an unsatisfied customer?**

This open-ended question gives you the chance to see how the candidate reacts under stress. Many candidates have very poor people skills, yet are so unaware of their own deficiencies that they sincerely believe that they are an empathetic person, when in reality they may be withdrawn and nerdish.

 **Top Answer**

The best answer to this question should include references to identifying with the problem, an eagerness to act to correct the problem, and a sincere willingness to help.

*I emphasized with the customer.*

*I tried to get them satisfaction as quickly as possible.*

*I was able to not take the issue personally and kept a professional and sympathetic demeanor.*

**? What is the description of your ideal job?**

This question is designed to allow the candidate to express their job goals and interests in tangible terms. The answer is not as important as their demeanor.

The best job applicants will not say what they think you want to hear and will feel free to express their personal values as they relate to the workplace.

**Top Answer**

The best answers to this question will be highly detailed with examples and illustrations of their ideal situation. Some of the best (and most honest) answers might include:

*I want to work in a stress-free environment where everybody has a team spirit and job goals are easily achievable.*

*My ideal job would be working in a job where I had total responsibility for an important area so that I could work on my team-building skills.*

*My ideal job would be working for an employer that valued initiative and gave me the freedom to pursue profitable avenues for the business.*

**?   What questions do you have?**

This is the signal for the candidate to show you their insights into the operations of your company.

The best answers should include references to how they could maximize your company productivity and they should avoid mention of company benefits and work environment. There is plenty of time to ask those types of questions after you have been offered the job.

The next chapter will go over the questions that a good job candidate will ask and the following chapter will review inappropriate questions that a candidate should never ask at an initial interview.

---

# Questions Candidates Ask

CHAPTER

## Learning about the Company

A job interview is a two-way street and the candidate should always use the interview as an opportunity to ask questions that may affect their propensity to accept the job offer.

A candidate should never ask a question simply for the sake of banter. Each question they ask should have personal value and they should only ask questions when they are invited to do-so by the interviewer. Remember, they are free to conduct their own interview after they have been offered the job!

Regardless of personal interest, there are some questions that every job applicant should ask. These questions show insight into the dynamics of employment and show that they are aware of the pitfalls of poor job opportunities.

- What is the attrition (turnover) rate?

- Why is this job open? Did someone quit?

- What are my opportunities for advancement?

- Am I expected to work more than 40 hours per week? If so, how many extra hours per week?

- What are the biggest challenges facing this department?

- What is your timeframe for making a decision?

> **?** **What is the attrition (turnover) rate?**

The answer to this question can be an important gauge of the type of employer your company will be. Low attrition shows employee loyalty seemingly because you are an employer who values the institutional knowledge of their employees and makes a sincere attempt to keep employees for long periods of time.

> **?** **Why is this job open? Did someone quit?**

This can be a loaded question and you must answer honestly. If the candidate accepts the position and later learns they are the latest in a string of unsatisfied employees, they may have a legal cause of action against your company for employment fraud.

> **?** **What are my opportunities for advancement?**

This is a great question because it gives you a chance to sell the company to a hot candidate. For those candidates who are unlikely to be extended an offer, this is not an important question.

> **?** **Am I expected to work more than 40 hours per week? If so, how many extra hours per week?**

Again, this is a very important question and one to be answered honestly. The overall cost of hiring is high and you don't want to be in a situation where you promised minimal overtime and your new employee is working 60 hours a week from the start. You may find yourself looking to fill this position again because your new star quit due to burnout.

---

? **What are the biggest challenges facing this department?**

---

This shows that the candidate has a genuine interest in the job and is concerned about their potential to find fulfilling work.

You should provide an honest assessment of the current situation in your department, the areas of weakness and be very detailed about your expectations regarding the performance of the new employee.

---

? **What is your timeframe for making a decision?**

---

This is a legitimate question, and one that you will likely hear from all your candidates. Again, an honest answer is appropriate.

# What a Candidate Should Never Ask

## Best of the Worst

While asking questions is a sign of candidate interest, the candidate should be very careful not to make assumptions and ask inappropriate questions. For example, any savvy job candidate knows that pay and benefits are usually determined during negotiations following a job offer, and the interviewer may not be in a position to discuss specific remuneration items such as pay and vacation time.

They should never assume that they have the job, and should avoid questions that make it appear that they are more interested in compensation than providing value to your company.

Too many questions about company benefits are always in bad taste. They should know that if they are offered the job, they will have an opportunity to review the compensation and benefit packages. The interview is not the right time to discuss these matters.

Some of the worst questions that I have heard from job candidates include these gems:

- How often do I get paid?
- Do you offer tuition reimbursement?
- Do you offer paid medical leave?
- When would I start?
- How much paid vacation do I get?

---

- Is it OK if I take two weeks off before I start?

---

**?  How often do I get paid?**

This is inappropriate because it indicates financial insecurity. As a general rule, lower wage un-salaried employees are paid weekly or bi-weekly while salaried employees are paid bi-weekly or monthly.

---

**?  Do you offer tuition reimbursement?**

It is never appropriate to discuss benefits until the candidate has been offered the job. If this question comes up, you may say that the details of the compensation and benefits package will be discussed in details with the successful candidate.

---

**?  Do you offer paid medical leave?**

This is not only inappropriate but is considered a major red-flag by some hiring managers. Any job candidate who is concerned with such matters may be disguising a serious medical condition.

---

**?  When would I start?**

This question is extremely presumptuous and may indicate a lack of good judgment and tact. All savvy candidates understand that these issues can all be negotiated after an offer is extended.

---

> **?**    **How much paid vacation do I get?**

Again, this is an inappropriate question because the amount of vacation may not be known at this stage. You and the HR department have a huge amount of flexibility in offering vacation time, and this figure is often used as a bargaining chip after the job offer has been extended.

> **?**    **Is it OK if I take two weeks off before I start?**

Again, this is a presumptuous question and one that is not appropriate for the initial on-site interview. Any job candidate who would ask this type of question during an initial interview may have personal issues that may prevent them from performing up to expectations. Further, this candidate may be asking for additional time so that they can take your hiring offer letter to other prospective employers. For obvious reasons, this type of employee should be avoided.

## Just for fun

If the interview is going poorly and the job candidate is certain they would not take the job, they may try to have some fun with you and deliberately ask some job-killer questions.

If the job candidate has self-confidence and wants to see how you react to absurd questions, you may see questions like these.

Some of my favorites include:

- Do you have an on-site Psychiatrist?

---

- Does your company support my Constitutional right to keep and bear arms?

- Would there be a problem if I spread the word about Jesus at work?

- What does the company Horoscope predict for next year's earnings?

- What is your long-term disability plan?

- Is there a bar near the office?

- How many warnings to you give before firing people?

Next, let's wrap-up the book and discuss what happens after the job offer has been extended and the candidate evaluates you and your work environment.

# After the Job Offer

## Evaluating the Employer

Once the candidate has secured a job offer, the interview process is only half completed. Now they must re-visit the interview process and determine if the job is right for them.

As we discussed in Chapter 11, this is the proper time for the candidate to ask detailed questions about their start time, pay, benefits, vacation, and work environment.

*Now it's your turn to be targeted with tough questions!*

After the job offer is extended the candidate is in a position to negotiate all aspects of the offer. Of course, pay and most benefits are normally hard to change, but adding another week to vacation can commonly be achieved.

At this point the savvy job candidate will ask the tough questions to determine if the job will be suitable for them. Aside from the obvious issues of pay and benefits, the job candidate is most likely concerned with you, their new supervisor.

## Evaluating you!

The candidates working relationship with you is one of the most important aspects of their job and the single most important factor in their long-term happiness on the job.

As a refresher, we can categorize all employees, both managers and workers, into three broad personality areas:

- The Scientist Employee/Supervisor
- The Gung-Ho Employee/Supervisor
- The Empathetic Employee/Supervisor

If your personality is significantly different from the candidate it does not necessarily mean that the job is a bad fit.

However, dissatisfaction with management is one of the top reasons for employee attrition, so the job candidate's final interview before accepting the position should be to ensure that the two of you will be able to enter a productive and satisfying long-term working relationship.

# Getting Along on the Job

By themselves, any of these three management personality types do an effective job. However, the problems begin when you have a personality conflict with the candidate.

*Find employees with complementary personalities.*

As you might expect, there are times when conflict arises between supervisors and employees, and it is interesting to hear employees complain about the shortcomings of their boss. Here is a synopsis of the complaints that I commonly hear:

## Complaints from the Scientist employee

The Scientist employee tolerates and likes an Empathetic supervisor, but has a real problem with the Gung-Ho supervisor.

The Scientist employee feels that the Gung-Ho supervisor is a "loose cannon" and cannot understand their impatience and disregard for detail. Secretly, the Scientist employee thinks that the Gung-Ho supervisor is dangerous, and cringes at their propensity to rush into everything.

## Complaints from the Gung-Ho employee

The Gung-Ho employee sees Empathetic supervisors as being lax and slow and also faults them for having highly misplaced priorities, maybe because they put family before work.

However, they have a much bigger problem with the Scientist supervisor, whom they see as rigid and overly cautious. Secretly, the Gung-Ho employee thinks that the Scientist supervisor should "get a life" and stop wasting time proving theories.

## Complaints from the Empathetic employee

Privately, the Empathetic employee does not understand the high dedication of the Scientist supervisor and Gung-Ho supervisor, but they would never say that out loud because it might cause conflict or hurt feelings.

# Conclusion

Again, these supervisor personality types are just my observations, and they are not based on any one individual, living or dead. If I am on target, I would love to hear from you, and I welcome any feedback or suggestions on how to improve my model.

# Appendix

## References

Hunter, J and Hunter, R, 1984, *'Validity and Utility of Alternative Predictors of Job Performance'*, Psychological Bulletin, 96:72-98

Poundstone W, 2003 *'How Would You Move Mount Fuji?: Microsoft's Cult of the Puzzle – How the World's Smartest Companies Select the Most Creative Thinkers'*, Little Brown & Company.

Willingham, W and Strickland J, 1962, *'Conversion Tables for Otis Gamma and Scholastic Aptitude Test,'* Personnel and Guidance Journal, 41(4), 1962, 356-358.

# Appendix

## Quiz for Computer Skills

Applicant's Name: _____

### General Skills:

1. You are developing a presentation for a new series of books. What tool would you use to create your presentation?

   _____

2. You need to sum a series of numbers in column A of an Excel spreadsheet, from cells 20 through 40, and place the result in cell A42. What equation would you place in cell A42?

   _____

3. You have a file document to send to an author that is too large for regular e-mail attachments. How would you get the document to the author?

   _____

   _____

4. Web pages may have many types of image files (e.g. jpg). List as many as you can, and describe their purpose.

_____

_____

_____

_____

5. Please provide as many font names as you know. For extra credit, list their specific uses for print matter and web pages.

_____

_____

_____

_____

_____

6. Describe the purpose of PDF files.

_____

_____

7. Describe the process (commands or mouse-clicks) for cutting and pasting text from one application to another.

_____

_____

_____

_____

8. Your PC "hangs" and you cannot get any open applications to respond. What should you do?

_____

_____

9. Briefly describe the purpose of the Windows registry.

_____

_____

_____

_____

10. Describe some things that you can do in the Control Panel.

_____

_____

_____

_____

_____

## Internet Skills:

1. What is considered to be the best search engine?

_____

_____

2. Develop a search query to locate publishers of children's book publishers in Shanghai China:

_____

_____

3. List some common tools that are used to publish web pages on the Internet.

_____

_____

_____

4. Describe the purpose of FTP.

_____

_____

_____

5. Name some ways (techniques, products) to protect your PC from Internet viruses.

_____

_____

_____

6. You are viewing a web page and want to see the source code for the page. How would you do this?

_____

_____

_____

7. Define the following Internet terms:

Flash: _____

HTML: _____

Java: _____

URL: _____

IP Address: _____

## MS-Word Skills:

1.  Describe the purpose of a DOT file.

_____

_____

_____

A DOT file is a document template that is used to provide standard headers, footers, and font types for new Word documents

2.  You need to send a document to a copy editor and you want to be able to have a record of all their changes.  How would you do this?

_____

_____

_____

3.  You have a wide document that you need to print sideways. How would you do this?

_____

_____

_____

4. You need to change the font size for all text of type "~Body Text." How would you do this?

_____

_____

_____

5. How would you select an entire word document?

_____

_____

_____

# Index

## About Don Burleson

*Donald K. Burleson* is the bestselling author of more than 30 books and is the CEO of a successful consulting company. Over the past two decades, Burleson has interviewed hundreds of job candidates and he is used by major corporations to interview and screen job applicants.

With advanced college degrees in Social Psychology and Business Administration, Burleson is a frequent speaker at International conferences and an opinion leader in hiring techniques.

A former Adjunct Professor, Don Burleson has written 32 books, published more than 100 articles in National Magazines, and serves as Editor-in-Chief of Oracle Internals, Senior Consulting Editor for DBAZine and Series Editor for Rampant TechPress. Don is a popular lecturer and teacher and is a frequent speaker at OracleWorld and other international database conferences.

In addition to his services as a consultant, Don is also active in charitable programs to aid visually impaired individuals. Don pioneered a technique for delivering tiny pigmy horses as guide animals for the blind and manages a non-profit corporation called the Guide Horse Foundation dedicated to providing Guide horses to blind people free-of-charge. The web site for The Guide Horse Foundation is www.guidehorse.org.

# About Mike Reed

When he first started drawing, Mike Reed drew just to amuse himself. It wasn't long, though, before he knew he wanted to be an artist.

Today he does illustrations for children's books, magazines, catalogs, and ads. He also teaches illustration at the College of Visual Art in St. Paul, Minnesota. Mike Reed says, "Making pictures is like acting — you can paint yourself into the action." He often paints on the computer, but also draws in pen and ink and paints in acrylics. He feels that learning to draw well is the key to being a successful artist.

Mike is regarded as one of the nation's premier illustrators and is the creator of the popular "Flame Warriors" illustrations at **www.flamewarriors.com**. A renowned children's artist, Mike has also provided the illustrations for dozens of children's books.

Mike Reed has always enjoyed reading. As a young child, he liked the Dr. Seuss books. Later, he started reading biographies and war stories. One reason why he feels lucky to be an illustrator is because he can listen to books on tape while he works. Mike is available to provide custom illustrations for all manner of publications at reasonable prices. Mike can be reached at **www.mikereedillustration.com**.

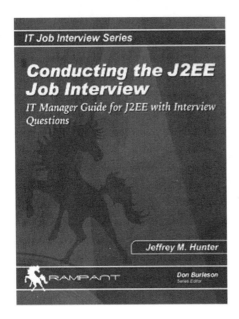

**Conducting the J2EE Job Interview**

*IT Manager Guide for J2EE with Interview Questions*

*Jeffrey M. Hunter*

ISBN 0-9744355-9-7

Retail Price $16.95 / £10.95

This book is the accumulated observations of the author's interviews with hundreds of job candidates. The author provides useful insights into what characteristics make a good J2EE programmer and offers his accumulated techniques as an aid to interviewing a J2EE programmer job candidate.

This handy guide has a complete set of J2EE job interview questions and provides a complete method for accurately assessing the technical abilities of J2EE job candidates. By using J2EE job interview questions that only an experienced person knows, your application developers can ask the right interview questions and fill your J2EE job with the best qualified J2EE developer.

**www.Rampant-Books.com**